EAT WRITE

Food, Work, Love, Loss

by Pam Felcher

Copyright © 2015 Pamela Felcher
All rights reserved.
ISBN-13: 978-1522705178
ISBN-10: 1522705171

DEDICATION

To my mom Rita and anyone else who has the patience to read my work. To Rocky, the ever patient. And to Dan, who edits with a vengeance.

CONTENTS

1	Hi, I'm Pam	1
2	A Valentine's Story	5
3	The Empress of Ice Cream	6
4	Frankenstein and Myrrh	9
5	In the Chips	11
6	What'd Ya Expect? Chopped Liver?	14
7	Reflections on Easter and Passover	16
8	Dreamgirls and Ophelia	18
9	La Dolce Vita	20
10	Happy Graduation	23
11	A Widow's Guide to Recovery	25

1 HI, I'M PAM

My husband Mike points out that the room goes silent as I watch a quivering, gooey strand of icing bridge a hunk of pastry being pried apart by delicate hands in an Entenmann's commercial. And when a pool of thick, rich Dove chocolate swirls around and folds itself magically over a brick of vanilla ice cream, my eyes glaze over. Then, when the caramel, nutty chocolate of a Milky Way is fully exposed in delectable close-up, my jaw goes slack. He tells me to face it: these commercials are, for me, like watching porn. Yes, I embarrassedly admit that I have fallen prey to the seductive enticement of sugary things.

At precisely 2pm every day, I find myself combing through my classroom, my desk, my closet, my cabinets, where I have squirreled away the many chocolates that my students have given to me for Halloween, Christmas, Valentine's Day, or, hell, just because they like me. I have enormous chocolate lips in red cellophane (the card signed with the kids' new vocabulary words, "To the *svelte behemoth*, Ms. Felcher"); giant and mini almond chocolate Hershey Kisses; gorgeous Leonidas 100% pure cocoa butter Belgian Chocolates in their trademark tiny gold box; half-pound Hershey plain, almond, and semisweet bars; Barnes and Noble Godiva and tiny See's boxes (I must say, whoever thought of blending my greatest pleasures, chocolate and reading, definitely got it right!).

Unfortunately, the Russell Stover's and Whitman Sampler's cloying morsels leave me with an itchy palate, but even that doesn't stop me. And Godiva (which one of my students calls "Go, Diva!") is hard to pass up. More often than I should admit, I have emerged from my closet with a telltale chocolate smear on my face and have raised my arm and said to a room full of students – head bowed, of course – "Hi, I'm Pam. I'm an addict." Without missing a beat, they respond in that supportive singsong, "Hi, Pam." They know.

Yet, despite the seemingly endless supply the kids provide, the one chocolate for which I constantly yearn and which the kids (or anyone) would probably be too embarrassed to buy as a gift, the one chocolate that has not disappointed me since I first met it as a preteen, the one chocolate that patently exposes my purely pedestrian tastes is the Reese's Peanut Butter Cup.

Sure, I buy the occasional bag of M&M Peanuts or M&M Almonds (for health reasons, naturally), but the Reese's Peanut Butter Cup is the real thing: salt and sweet, smooth and rough, the perfect balance of dense, discreet, yet blended flavors and textures. It is a dependable chocolate, yet it is always a surprise.

It's the *People Magazine* of chocolates, right there in the impulse rack at the grocery or drugstore checkout line, ready for me to convince myself it's vacation. So why not grab that *People* and indulge in an equally lurid and maybe vulgar but always delicious chocolate.

Pam Felcher

2   A VALENTINE'S STORY

I met my husband Mike in Paris, and, no, it was not like that. He was visiting his sister and I was a friend of hers traveling through Europe. Well, one day she and I convinced him to go shopping with us. I needed an extra layer because it was a colder summer than I had anticipated, and I had not brought the correct wardrobe. A nearby shop made elaborate and exquisite batik sarongs that easily doubled as elegant wraps, scarves, shawls (keep in mind, this is pre-pashmina).

I looked through the piles of these colorful garments in search of one that was more earth tone--the kind of girl I am--but Mike picked up this bright red pattern, held it up to me and said, "This would look pretty on you." Well, I had never heard the words "pretty" and you (meaning "me"!) together in a sentence before, so I took notice.

Of course, he was probably humoring me, more eager to get to the café for a beer than anything else. Who knew that such expedience would lead to a 14-year marriage. Gives new meaning to the expression, "Flattery will get you nowhere."

3   THE EMPRESS OF ICE CREAM

For most of my dad's young life, he lived above and worked at Felcher's, his parents' neighborhood candy store and lunch counter, tucked between P and G's Bar and Grill and Simpson's Hardware Store on Amsterdam Avenue between 73rd and 74th Streets. Christopher Morley would watch my dad as a tiny boy play in front of that store and immortalized him as "the man of the future" in his novel *Kitty Foyle.*

Throughout college and law school, my dad scooped ice cream and served sandwiches at this lunch counter while his then girlfriend, my mother, perched herself on a stool out front, eating fudgicles and unwittingly enticing much of the passing parade, including several of the 1950s NY Giants. I can still see the scoop my father kept from Felcher's—the well-worn wooden handle and scored thumb press that pushed the slim metal band that would release the perfect scoop, every time.

When I was a kid growing up in Riverdale, my dad would take us to Goldman's Luncheonette on Johnson Avenue, where I discovered the unbeatable combination of tuna on rye and chocolate malteds. That I could buy

Archie Comics on the way out was another boon.

But once my dad moved back to the city, sadly without my mom, my sister, and me, I surprisingly discovered an ice cream that I did not like, an ice cream I believed to be one of the staples of divorced fathers everywhere: Haagen Dazs Rum Raisin. All my pleasurable associations with ice cream could have been erased by the shifts in my home life, accompanied by that brief flavor lapse. Fortunately, my tastes are not as ephemeral as the treat itself.

During my teen years, Carvel and Dairy Queen both opened up in my neighborhood. Dairy Queen, on Riverdale Avenue; Carvel, on Johnson. I am not sure whether it was my loyalty to the long-gone Johnson Avenue Goldman's, but for me Carvel won that competition. I could not get enough of those Flying

Saucers, soft-serve chocolate dipped cones, and Tom Carvel's fanciful ice cream cakes (what an inspired combo that is, by the way, ice cream AND cake!). Then came the ultimate revelation: Baskin-Robbins. I had heard about their ice cream for years, every time my Grandma would return from a visit to my Aunt in Ventura, California, who got through her pregnancies by practically living at her local Baskin-Robbins.

 Once those famed 31 flavors landed in my neighborhood, sugar cones filled with two scoops of Jamoca Almond Fudge had me scrambling for all the loose change I could muster. I'd like to say that Ben and Jerry's and Hagen Dazs and McConnell's and Cold Stone are my other favorites, but I would be lying. My tastes are far too common. The Chocolate Cherry Overload that Breyer's has given us feels redemptive because of the large chunks of healthful cherry and dark chocolate, and Thrifty coffee ice cream-- topped with Fox's U-Bet Chocolate Syrup, naturally--can perk up even the dullest day. And I think I may have gained all my winter weight the summer I discovered Trader Joe's Mint Chocolate Chip.

 Wallace Stevens famously claims, "The only emperor is the emperor of ice-cream," and I say what an empire it is!

4   FRANKENSTEIN AND MYRRH?

When I was a kid, say about 7 or 8, my dad brought home a holiday gift that was emblematic of his personality: a foot high Frankenstein's monster, standing on a metal pedestal, dressed all in black with a large and distorted plastic chalk-green head decorated with bumpy zigzag cherry-red scars. His black gash of a mouth spread across his face in a faint smile.

The best part about this Frankenstein was the little switch on his back. At my father's insistence, I pushed that switch and the monster with his arms outstretched, started to shimmy back and forth and side to side. Then my sister and I could hear a little grinding sound, and click, off slid his pants. There he was, Frankenstein's monster, no longer shimmying, but standing still on his pedestal in red and white striped boxers. That faint smile of his now revealed a slight insouciance. Our gleeful giggles were overpowered by my father's healthy, if sinister, chortle. To this day I am still not sure whether he loved the toy or our reaction to it. Knowing him, though, my money's on the toy.

Cut to my marriage of several more years than I had ever expected. It's that end of year holiday season that puts everyone into a tizzy, and my husband brings me a gift that he cannot wait to give to me. Nope, no velvet covered satin or sky blue boxes in this house. I open the long rectangular box to find Mel Brook's version of Frankenstein's monster: a foot-tall Peter Boyle, tinted to look as if he just walked out of a black and white movie – skin perfectly gray, felt coat and pants an ensemble of black and gray, hair (despite the male pattern baldness) perfectly black, as are his lips, eyes, handcuffs.

Yes, this monster comes with accessories and removable limbs. I can take off the hand that clutches the bowl that could never quite catch the soup that blind Gene Hackman ladled out to him, and I can replace it with the hand with the burning thumb – again a result of another hilarious Hackman gaffe. This monster does not shimmy, but all I have to do is look at him and remember his heartfelt and ridiculous rendition of "Putting on the Ritz" and the laughter bubbles up in me.

So now it's the holidays again, and while many women out there are hoping for something that sparkles and commemorates love and joy, I am too. . . You think it will be Igor this time? Or should I say, EYE-gor?

5   IN THE CHIPS

My dad lived part-time in Sag Harbor and made the drive from the city every weekend in every type of weather. I would visit him and my stepmother every summer, and we'd stay put for the weekend, usually poolside. My dad and I would swim back and forth and read books and nap. He would do his Sunday puzzle and I would nudge him for clues; I would read books he gave me and he would nudge me about which part I was up to. To me, my dad was part Phillip Roth and part John Updike, so I read Phillip Roth and John Updike. Because we both loved to punctuate headier reading with murder mysteries, he would toss me his copies of Lee Child or Lawrence Block, and I would gobble them up like candy. I still have the water-swollen copy of Annie Proulx's *Shipping News* that he accidentally tossed into the pool in order to save me from a hovering bee, and I remember how he had said he envied my getting to read it for the first time.

But what would any return home to the family be without the requisite favorite foods? Besides the inevitable Saturday night lobster, the most memorable part of the summer, food-wise, in addition to the muskmelons and the corn and potatoes and other fresh fare at the roadside markets, were the little blue and white checkered bags of chocolate-chip cookies that one could find only at Kathleen's Bake Shop.

Admittedly, this was not the first time a local food put its delicious stamp on my summer. There were Friendly's Fribbles, the first triple-thick chocolate milkshakes I ever had, and Freihofer's small, chewy chocolate chip cookies in the white box with the red label, both the delicacies of summers spent at camps in Massachusetts and the Adirondacks. Kathleen's, these flat, crisp, salty, chocolatey cookies in the tradition of summer snacks past soon became an essential part of my summer-visit food routine.

Unfortunately, these cookies were Hamptons exclusive, though I think I found them once in a boutique snack shop near the Hampton Jitney stop in the East 50ies, and maybe I found them once at Zabar's. So each year I would stash bags of Kathleen's 15 or so cookies, which came stacked in two separate cellophane covered plastic trays, into my suitcase so I could enjoy a part of Sag Harbor once back in L.A. I am not one to eat an entire pint of ice cream or a bag of cookies all by my lonesome, but Kathleen's rare, perfect, salty-sweet chocolate-chip cookies were impossible to stop eating once you got started. That it was also impossible to rewrap them made the logic of eating all of them at once (well at least one tray's worth) easy to swallow, so to speak.

Just when I got used to this annual splurge of mine, one summer Kathleen's cookies disappeared. Apparently, Kathleen King had lost the rights to use her own name on her bakeshop and poof went the cookies.

Shortly afterwards, my dad passed away, as did my summers in Sag Harbor.

It's funny how just when you think memories are solidly encased in an immutable past, something happens to remind you that memory is a living, self- defining power, and what better than a familiar food to trigger this capacity.

Recently, I was shopping at my local Gelson's, and right in front of me in the cookie aisle, there they were,

7-ounce, light-green bags of Tate's all-natural chocolate-chip cookies. I had heard over the years that Kathleen had renamed her brand.

One bite and there I was again in Sag Harbor, the sun on my face, my dad tapping his tooth with his pen, working the puzzle. Just delicious.

6   WHAT'D YA EXPECT? CHOPPED LIVER?

I think it was Joan Rivers who joked about an epitaph that would suit her: "I'd rather be here than in the kitchen!" Or was her line, "If God wanted women to cook, he would have given them aluminum hands?" Either way, my mother has lived by both of these lines her whole life…well, at least for as long as I lived with her as a kid. So imagine my sister's and my surprise when one sunny Sunday morning, while in our early and mid-teens, we awoke to a basket of picture-perfect bran muffins. Astounding.

    We wondered what had suddenly possessed this woman whose disdain for the kitchen was evinced weekly by small hamburgers formed in the palm of her hand, slightly bulging in the center, tapered at the edges, and so over cooked that they would crumble into gray, gristly pebbles. To make matters worse, my mom had a fondness for ketchup as the panacea for all cooking ills, so to this day I don't touch the stuff. Before one of our holiday dinners, a favorite cousin of hers placed rolls of TUMS at every place setting. Her reputation preceded her.

    My sister and I stared at the basket, the plump brown muffins perched in a perfect cluster. "Should we?" we tittered. We each plucked one of the muffins from its nest and peeled off the paper wrapper. Tentatively, we put our lips to the muffin tops, then we took big bites. Mouths full, eyes wide…the shock was instant.

    Nothing about these beautiful specimens was palatable, so we immediately spit out the bites we had taken and even wiped our tongues to remove any traces of the dreadful things.

When our mother awoke, we asked her about the muffins. Was she was trying to poison us? She laughed as she explained that she may have forgotten to add sugar and *might* have added measures of salt instead. Of course she did.

This is not to say that my mother's cooking is a total loss. She makes a pretty good Thanksgiving turkey, spoons the cranberry sauce from the can carefully enough to keep the ribbing intact, browns the marshmallows and yams perfectly, and follows the green bean casserole recipe to the letter. In fact, this is the meal she makes every holiday because she does it so well.

The best part of the meal is the chopped liver appetizer she makes from the turkey liver. In the solid wood chopping bowl she got from the hardware store when I was a toddler, she chops up the liver, hard boiled eggs, onions she cannot help burning, and throws in a little mayo instead of the typical schmaltz. Unlike much chopped liver, which is usually as dense as caulk, this chopped liver is salty, flavorful but not too rich, moist, and loosely constructed. Some may consider it a mistake, but to me it's perfect.

7 REFLECTIONS ON EASTER AND PASSOVER

As a secular Jew married to a lapsed Catholic, I guess you could say that religion for me has always been a spectator sport. I know that when Easter is upon us, my catholic friends (yes, I keep the lower case because I mean those who embrace all things) celebrate the resurrection of Jesus Christ with a holiday whose name is derived from the name of a goddess associated with spring. I guess that explains all the chocolate fertility symbols. I also know that this Christian holiday normally coincides with Passover because the Last Supper was a Passover Seder, and we all know how that went.

Given my distance from all the ritualized fun, I have a few questions for the Easter Egg enthusiast. Do they suck the egg out of the shell? How? And if so, who has a steady enough hand to paint these fragile canvases? Or are the eggs all hardboiled? Or worse, are they plastic? Well, I suppose that's not worse if they are filled with sugary, gummy, or chocolate treats.

And for Passover enthusiasts, why aren't there five questions, the last one being, "Why is this Seder taking so long?"

The last Seder to which I was invited (and given the questions I ask here, you can see why I am not on more guest lists) sat 25 people. Because I am a NY transplant with no Seder-providing family out here, a student had invited me. I brought my husband Mike, who is no slouch when it comes to handling alcohol (all that altar boy training, he tells me). He perked up when I told him that the meal begins with the guests reading passages from the Passover story, and each passage is punctuated by a little bowl of wine.

So there we were, many, many gulps of wine later, the last to read at this huge table. Just as the reading prompts were headed our way, Mike leaned into me like a tree falling (he's not a tiny guy) to tell me he's "ha-ha-hammered." Naturally. All that sugary sweet wine was not exactly what he was expecting.

Later, after the hangover dissipated, he said, "That's why Jesus' first miracle was making wine! Only cough syrup should be cherry flavored!"

Even though I am essentially an outsider, for me these holidays are magic the way putting a glass to a wall and hearing the sounds next door is magic. We may not apprehend the specific sounds, but the general rhythms move us all.

8   DREAMGIRLS AND OPHELIAS

I live in West Hollywood, where Halloween is like a national holiday – arrangements for street closures have been made well in advance, and people from all over will come watch the flagrant and the flamboyant, the political and the theatrical, the absurd and the sublime march along Santa Monica Boulevard, from La Cienega to Doheny. Candy is not an integral part of this spectacle, and frankly that's the only thing that rankles me about it.

One year, the Wicked Witch of the West wheeled along the Boulevard with an enormous crystal ball that housed terrorized miniatures of Dorothy, Toto, and the other Oz pilgrims, all cowering on the yellow brick road within her bubble. Another year, there were several Menendez brothers, wearing blood covered v-neck sweaters and conservative haircuts. Then another year, there were groups of huddled Titanic musicians playing desperately as their ship was sinking (or, I should say, as the parade was passing them by).

Once there was a Humpty Dumpty, sitting on his wall. The guy had painted his face white, rimmed his eyes with red liner, painted his lips red, and glued little tiny arms to his cheeks. He put a body sized, cardboard brick wall under his chin and would walk a few steps then plant himself, egg resting on wall, as still as a chocolate bar. People would approach him cautiously and stare at him. He wouldn't even blink. Creepy. His little hands could have at least held little Hershey's Kisses for the curious passersby.

Of course, every year there are the requisite six-foot tall, sherbet-wigged airline hostesses with their sky-blue Pan Am bags and uniforms, à la Boeing, Boeing. And who can miss the enormous, red and white sequined West Hollywood cheerleaders and their muscular calves, marching like candy canes down the Boulevard. Milkmen and mechanics, cops and cowboys, nuns and priests fill out the crowd, as do Cher, Bette Midler, and the Dreamgirls – all looking like cotton-candy confections.

When the holiday would fall on a school day, I would get a double dose of parading alter-egos. I taught at a Music Academy, where kids wore costumes almost daily. I offered extra credit to the kids who dressed up like the literary figures we were reading. This challenge brought out the sultry Hester Prynne and flower-laden Ophelia in some; the morose Hamlet and monstrous Grendel in others. The spectacle of Gatsbys and Daisys and Titanias and Bottoms warmed this English teacher's heart.

I suppose every costume, like every symbol in a dream, is a revelation of an inner-self. Or maybe it's a reflection of the way we think we are seen. Or maybe it reflects the way we want to be seen.

Well, I always wear the same costume, a witch's hat, so I'll let my students decide what they are seeing. Whatever they think I might be revealing to them, I hope they give me candy.

9   LA DOLCE VITA

As I have mentioned, I am a teacher in the LAUSD and the budget cuts cost me dearly. I lost the auxiliary class I taught for nine years. Though the class added the stress of an extra preparation and thirty-five more papers to grade each week, it also padded my wallet, which made it a little easier for me to inure myself to teaching four 90-minute classes every day with only two brief scheduled breaks.

Gates and locks define the boundaries of the campus and these gates and locks are not to be opened until the school day ends, so this means that for nine years, I have been almost literally chained to my desk.

Not once in nine years have I ever "met a friend for lunch" or gone off campus to "grab a bite." Since there is really no time to do anything but teach my classes, answer student questions, and make small talk in the bathroom line, I practically live in my little isolated realm.

I have packed my little island with the essential modern conveniences like a fridge stocked with berries, Greek yogurt, organic peanut butter, whole grain bread, cheese, water, juice; a kettle to boil water for coffee and the morning's oatmeal; and an iPhone, so I can enjoy the promise of at least some contact with the outside world during those two luxurious breaks I get. A colleague once asked whether I was hiding a Murphy bed in my book closet.

This week, on my way back to class during the morning break, I got a call from a friend who asked what I was doing for lunch. The question, alive with the thrill of leisure and adulthood, might normally have crushed my spirits. Instead, I paused for a second and remembered that because I lost my auxiliary class, I am actually free two out of three afternoons a week. This was going to be one of those afternoons.

So at 1:15 PM, during the lunch period, I did the previously unimaginable . . . I walked out of school "to meet a friend for lunch" to "grab a bite." Fortunately for me, Dolce Isola had opened its doors just up the street.

The bright red building with its red and white striped awning and little ice-cream tables and chairs out front stands out like an oasis on an otherwise gray section of south Robertson Boulevard. Unlike the teacher's cafeteria offerings, their pastry case does not contain wilted tuna sandwiches on soggy wheat bread or Brillo Pad LAUSD coffee cake. Nope, this case is full of delectable treats like Mitzi's Earthquake chocolate cookies; Red Velvet cupcakes, topped with cream-cheese icing; lemon squares; chocolate croissants; tea scones; chocolate truffle tortes; and the Tarte tartin that I hear is the best anywhere. Just looking at the display should give anyone a sense of well being.

For lunch my friend and I first shared the homemade guacamole and filled homemade tortillas--hot and satisfying--with the abundant avocado mixture. He opted for the Dolce Club Sandwich. I picked the Ivy Buffet: Normandy chicken salad, fresh tuna salad, pasta a la checca, and lo scogglio potato salad. Every bite delicious, particularly the potato salad, which, to my great joy, was more Mediterranean than American.

What is perhaps most exciting about Dolce Isola is the fact that it is the bakery for The Ivy restaurants. That means not only had I been sprung from my work confinement for the first time in nine years, and not only had I the chance to spend time with my dear friend, but I also got to enjoy a meal that was being similarly enjoyed in the tonier reaches of the same boulevard. I had briefly traded my little classroom island for the Dolce Isola and enjoyed every second of it--except I forgot to get dessert. Well. . . next time.

10 HAPPY GRADUATION

I have taught English for almost thirty years and the reading, planning, grading, and, yes, the teaching consume much of my waking time from August 28th until June 20th every year. I have never had children of my own, but I guess you could say I'm "the village." I have taught about 3200 students so far, ranging from the kids whose mothers clean homes to the kids whose moms employ the other moms.

I have taught future lawyers, doctors, rabbis, curators, filmmakers, poets, art historians, scientists, and I have taught future crack addicts, pregnant teens, suicides, and criminals. I have taught the ambitious and the indolent, the focused and the preoccupied, the optimistic and the pessimistic, the successful and the not so successful.
I draw lines and erase them; I support when it's hopeless; I assist and advise constantly; I make them laugh and I make them cry. I always hope to make them better, even when they want to feel worse. I always hope to make them stronger, even when they feel too weak to go on. They push back and I push harder.

Every year they fight me from August to December until they start to see a difference in their thinking and writing from January to March. The minute the calendar turns to April they grow increasingly nostalgic about all the fun they had and all they learned in my class. Then, before you can say Memorial Day, suddenly it's June, and I have to bid goodbye to yet another legion of potential lawyers, doctors, painters, drug addicts, cooks, housekeepers, writers, computer programmers, social workers, teachers, lab techs, producers, firemen, I could go on.

After I hug them at their graduation and tell them to keep in touch and I thank their parents for raising terrific kids. As I wave heartily at the last smiling face, a thick silence pervades the atmosphere. . . .Then. . . it's August.

So this piece is just to say, Happy Graduation Day to all my grads! Remember, I am always in your corner.

Love,

"The Village"

11   THE WIDOW'S GUIDE TO RECOVERY

My husband Mike passed away suddenly five years ago. A "catastrophic coronary event," I remember hearing before the doctor launched into the "We did everything we could" speech. I sat motionless in the Naugahyde chair in that dimly lit room they usher people into to tell them such things.

Mike was the guy who could put the caption on the cartoon we call life. I can still be felled by a wave of sadness when the world calls out for his wit, but it usually passes as the business of life encroaches and forces the sadness aside. If I've learned anything, it's that grief is not a linear process or a series of predictable steps. It comes and it goes, lingers or dusts by. It can overpower or gently remind. Now you see it; now you don't.

The second year into loss, the cycles of grief had given way to the flat, dark monotony of depression. Since action is my default response, I checked out inspirational websites for those contemplating putting themselves out of their own misery, and I downloaded into my iPhone Kindle any number of self-help books about depression and the powers of positive thinking. I answered every "Are you suffering from..." and "On a scale of 1-10..." quiz that the books offered.

My friends suggested that my trying to gain a little more perspective would help, but from their comments I could tell that depression long after the event sounded like self- absorption. My inability, or what may have seemed to be my unwillingness, to see things differently was making me difficult to be around. One friend told me to "Think of things for which you are grateful…" As if the depression would evaporate if I could just fill in the "Things about which to be grateful" column with enough to cancel out the "Self- Pity" column on life's general accounting sheet.

I even entertained the notion of medication, thinking that taking a daily pill would help me feel as if I were being proactive and not just wallowing in bad feelings. But just before I got to the prescription stage, my therapist asked me to name something I would love to do. At that moment a thin ray of some long-forgotten childhood dream pierced the darkness, and horseback riding popped into my head.

I told my therapist that I had ridden a bit when I was younger, so when I first moved to California decades ago, I had the fantasy that a horse and I would kick up dust as the mountains around us lit up orange in the glow of the setting sun. He told me to go online and search for lessons.

After about eight months of riding lessons, I graduated to a horse no one else would ride because he wasn't the nicest horse and had been suffering with arthritis, thrush, and laminitis. But I just needed to hear his name to know it was meant to be: Chutzpah! Here was the Jewish girl from the Bronx riding the American Saddlebred with the Jewish name and bad feet. The clincher came after our first lesson. As I was bent over to muck out his hooves, he bent down to nibble my rear end. I jumped up and cried, "Mike?!" only half joking.

In January it will be four years since I started riding Chutzpah and learning about the love and care of a horse. Anyone can feed a horse carrots and apples, but I discovered German Horse biscuits and Paddock Cakes, tiny moist cakes made of molasses, sweet feed, and flour, topped with peppermints.

Now, every time I groom Chutzpah, as I move from one side to the other to curry and brush him, I can smell the peppermint on his breath, and I myself can taste happiness.

ABOUT THE AUTHOR

Pam Felcher has been a teacher in Los Angeles for thirty years. She has taught in public and private school, university and yeshiva. Her essays and letters about education have appeared in various publications including the *Los Angeles Times*. The pieces that appear here have been featured in *oneforthetable.com*

Made in the USA
San Bernardino, CA
20 November 2018